D0337149

Series consultant: Dr Dorothy Rowe

The author and publisher would like to thank
the staff and pupils of the following schools for their help
in making this book: St Vincent de Paul Roman Catholic
School, Westminster; Mayfield Primary School,
Cambridge; Swavesey Village College, Cambridge.

A CIP catalogue record for this book
is available from the British Library.

ISBN 0-7136-6331-6

First paperback edition published 2002
First published in hardback in 1997 by
A & C Black Publishers Ltd
37 Soho Square, London W1D 3QZ
www.acblack.com

Text copyright © 1997 Althea Braithwaite
Photographs copyright © 1997 Charlie Best
Illustrations copyright © 1997 Conny Jude

Typeset in 15/19 pt Sabon Roman and
13/19 pt Futura Bold Oblique.

A & C Black uses paper produced with elemental
chlorine-free pulp, harvested from managed sustainable forests.

Printed in Hong Kong through Colorcraft Ltd.

Feeling Scared

Althea

**Photographs by
Charlie Best**

**Illustrations by
Conny Jude**

A & C Black · London

We all have things that make us frightened. Some of these things are real and some are just in our minds.

I get scared of going up to bed in the dark.

Shona says, "At night, when I hear lots of noises, I imagine that people are coming to get me. I know it's silly, but I can't help myself!"

I'm scared of thunderstorms. I hate the bangs and I'm sure I'll be struck by lightning.

What makes you scared?

Different people react to fear in different ways. Some people say they feel like running away, or just sinking into the ground.

I go cold and shivery.

My stomach churns and I feel queasy.

I used to go rigid when I saw a spider!

My mouth goes dry.

How do you feel when you get scared?

Everyone has been scared of the dark at some time in their life. Things can seem much more scary at night - you can feel very alone. Noises seem much louder when it's quiet.

"I kept having the same nightmare every night, and I was scared to go to sleep. I didn't tell my mum. I just said I wasn't tired and didn't want to go to bed."

Sam remembers, "I was scared of being upstairs alone. I used to try and get my brother to go and play on his computer, so someone else was upstairs too."

If I wake at night I still get frightened by the strange shadows on the walls.

The dreams that we have are jumbles of ideas, experiences and feelings that we have hidden during the day. So if you felt very angry, but didn't show it, the anger may be changed into a frightening monster in your dream. But dreaming about something doesn't make it happen.

Not everything that worries us makes us feel scared.
Sometimes we may just feel a bit nervous or worried about something.

Jan says, "I'm nervous when I plan to stay overnight with my friend. It's silly really because I always enjoy it when I'm actually there."

We went pond dipping and I fell in. I was scared because I can't swim and my boots were filling with water.

It's sensible to feel scared of things that are dangerous because you can take care to avoid them.

Someone who claims that they're never frightened is likely to take dangerous risks - like running across the road in front of a car.

Danny's always taking chances on his bike. He's been nearly knocked off twice this year already.

Have you ever frightened yourself on purpose?

At the fair, I went on a terrifying ride. I was sure I was going to fall out. It made me scream!

It can be fun to be scared of something. That's why we play scary games and clutch each other or scream when we hear a noise. When you are doing it you get really frightened, but when you stop you wish you could be scared again.

It's all right to want the thrills of being scared, when you know everything will be all right in the end. But if you end up really frightening yourself, it might be difficult to stop worrying just by telling yourself not to be silly.

When I'm reading a really exciting ghost story, I get scared, but I can't stop reading it.

New situations can sometimes be scary. If we don't know what's going to happen next, we don't know how to behave.

Shona says, "If someone I don't know, like a shopkeeper, is horrid to me, it makes me scared and I think the whole world is a dangerous place."

Sam says, "I get scared when I have to answer the phone. I don't know who it will be or whether I'll know what to say."

Ring, Ring

Jan remembers, "I was scared of going to my new school. I thought they would make me stand up and read, and I wouldn't be as good as the others."

Sometimes, even when you are scared stiff, it's difficult to admit it to close friends or to your parents. But often, when you do tell them what's scaring you, you may find that they feel the same way.

Many people feel frightened by things they cannot control.

When my parents have a row I'm scared that Dad will leave us, like my friend's dad did.

When my mum's ill in bed, I get frightened that she might die.

It doesn't help if someone says "Don't worry, it won't happen". We all know bad things do happen. But you can't stop bad things from happening by worrying about them.

It helps if we can learn to enjoy the present and not worry about things that are out of our control. We can stop ourselves from dwelling on worries by saying to ourselves, "I'm not going to think about that right now". It might help to think about something nice or tell yourself a story to take your mind off what's frightening you.

It's easy to become frightened that an awful thing is going to happen, when you don't have all the facts about something.

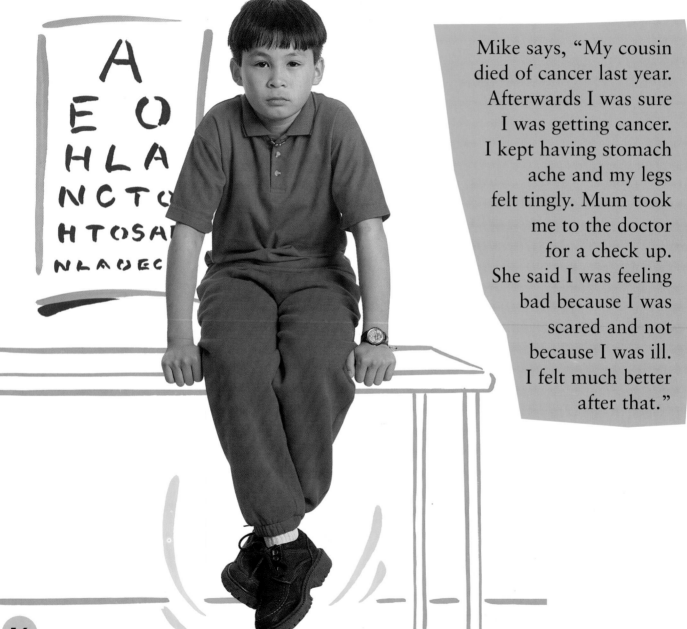

Mike says, "My cousin died of cancer last year. Afterwards I was sure I was getting cancer. I kept having stomach ache and my legs felt tingly. Mum took me to the doctor for a check up. She said I was feeling bad because I was scared and not because I was ill. I felt much better after that."

My friend has eczema. I thought I was going to get it too, because I used her towel. Then she told me that eczema isn't catching.

When you are scared of something and you don't know all the facts, it's a good idea to ask. You might be making yourself frightened over nothing.

17

There are lots of ways of stopping yourself from being scared.

When I'm in bed I shut my eyes and tell myself there's nothing to be frightened of. Then I think of something nice, like my birthday party.

Sam says, "I watched the spooky video that scared me over and over again, until it didn't frighten me anymore."

"When there is a storm I shut the curtains and turn up the TV - it cuts out most of the noise."

What do you do to stop yourself being frightened?

Over time, most of us find that we learn to cope with lots of different fears. After dealing with a scary experience once, it might not be so frightening next time round.

"I was scared when I was learning to ride a bike. I thought I would never be able to do it. I felt a fool each time I fell off. But after a while I got the hang of it. Now it doesn't feel like such a big deal at all!"

"I fell and cut my knee on some glass.
I was terrified I would have to have stitches.
We went to hospital and I did have stitches,
but it wasn't too bad."

Shona says,
"When I was younger,
I was scared of escalators.
I thought I might get caught
at the top and sucked in.
I know it's not possible, but
I still jump off when we get
to the top!"

When you talk about your fears you will find that other people have their own fears too.

Sometimes I'm just very scared without knowing why.

We all have these unexplained fears at times. Even your heroes, the people you most admire, feel frightened at times. You can't be courageous or brave if you never feel frightened.

I was asked to act in the school play. I was mega-scared. But I plucked up the courage and did it - and it was really good!

If you are scared and overcome a fear, you are braver than someone who is not frightened.

For teachers and parents
A note from Dorothy Rowe

Children often feel frightened but, sadly, adults often belittle a child's fears or ignore them. This happens sometimes because the adult thinks that the child's fears are not important and sometimes because the adult is also frightened but doesn't want to admit it. To help a child deal with fear, adults need to remember that our fear arises out of how we have interpreted a situation and that no two people ever interpret a situation in exactly the same way.

The starting point must be to find out how the child sees the situation. Even when the child's fears arise out of ignorance, being given the correct information will not necessarily reassure the child. Being told that you have a one in a million chance of getting cancer might not be interpreted by the child as good odds for staying well. After all, many adults think that one in fourteen million are good odds for winning the lottery!

Often a child's seemingly irrational fears, like fear of the dark, relate to the major issues we all face - death, losing someone we love, meeting people who might be hostile. There are no simple solutions to these issues but pretending that these issues aren't there won't make them go away. Through discussions with adults who can talk about how they get frightened and what they do to overcome their fears, children can work out practical ways of dealing with their fears and develop a philosophy of life based on the necessity of courage.

To start a discussion and get everyone involved, both you and the children could write a list of all the things that make you scared, then compare lists. Many people are frightened of the dark or of being alone at home. But people are sometimes scared of admitting their fears, in case they sound silly. Once one person has admitted to a fear it's much easier for others to do so too, and to talk about it.

Many ideas can be discussed page by page when going through the book again. The following points may prove useful starting points.

Page 6 Some children may have been threatened that they are being watched from on high, and if they are bad they will get their punishment in the end. This can seem very much more likely to happen in the dark.

Page 7 It may take a very long time to hear everyone's bad dreams and nightmares. Perhaps instead they should write about them or draw a picture.

Page 8 Some people are very unaware of the danger of their actions. It's important that the more cautious are not made to feel cowardly. Dare games can be very dangerous or even fatal, as accidents on railway lines have shown.

Page 14-15 Sadly, nasty things do happen at times. People are terrified of how they would cope and if they would survive if something awful happened. If someone you love and need dies or leaves you, you do survive in spite of the great unhappiness and pain.

Page 16-17 Adults also may need to learn the facts as they can sometimes instil fears into their children through lack of knowledge. Parents sometimes pass on their more general fears too. They may consistently portray the world as a dangerous place, in which no-one can be trusted, or 'worry about what the neighbours might say'. Children pick up their anxieties and may become fearful.

Pages 18-19 Maybe the child shouldn't be watching the scary video. It can be silly to frighten yourself unnecessarily. It's not cowardly to decide not to do things that make you frightened.

Page 22 We all have unexplained feelings of fear. It's important that we tell ourselves we are not going to be overwhelmed by them.

Further reading

Children may find it interesting and helpful to have a look at some of the following story books which also deal with the subject of feeling scared.

Joan Aiken
A Creepy Company
(Puffin, 1995)

Anthony Browne
The Tunnel
(Walker, 1992)

Richard McGilvray
Don't Climb Out of the Window Tonight
(Metheun, 1994)

Francesca Simon
What's That Noise?
(HodderHeadline, 1996)